MW00995139

CogAT® Screening Form
Practice Test
GRADE 5
LEVEL 11

Practice Questions from the CogAT
Form 7 / Form 8 Analogies Sections: Verbal/Picture
Analogies, Number Analogies, & Figure Matrices.

ISBN: 978-1-948255-89-9

Origins Publications
New York, NY, USA

email:info@originspublications.com

Origins Publications

Origins Publications helps students develop their higher-order thinking skills wh
also improving their chances of admission into gifted and accelerated-learn
programs.

Our goal is to unleash and nurture the genius in every student. We do this by
offering educational and test prep materials that are fun, challenging and provic
a sense of accomplishment.

Please contact us with any questions.

info@originspublications.com

Contents

Introduction to the CogAT® Screening Form

This book offers an overview of the types of questions on the CogAT® Level 11 Screening Form, test-taking strategies to improve performance, sample questions, and a full-length CogAT Screening Form practice test that students can use to assess their knowledge and practice their test-taking skills. It is important that you read this entire introduction!

Who Takes the CogAT® Level 11 Screening Form?

The CogAT Level 11 Screening Form is a test that is often used as an expedient yet reliable assessment tool or admissions test in 5th grade for entry into gifted and talented (GATE) programs and highly-competitive schools.

What is the Difference Between the CogAT® and the CogAT® Screening Form?

The CogAT Screening Form is a shorter version of the full length CogAT Form 7. The Screening Form contains only the analogies section of each battery: picture/verbal analogies, number analogies, and figure matrices. Some schools prefer the CogAT Screening Form, as the test offers a quality evaluation with a shorter administration time than the complete CogAT.

When Does the CogAT® Screening Form Test Take Place?

This depends on the school district you reside in or want to attend. Check with the relevant school/district to learn more about test dates and the application/ registration process.

CogAT® Level 11 Screening Form Overview

The CogAT Screening Form is a group-administered test that features only the analogies section of each of the three independent 'batteries': Verbal, Quantitative, and Nonverbal. It is designed to assess learned reasoning in these three areas, which experts believe are the areas most closely linked to academic achievement.

The CogAT Screening Form covers topics that students may not see in school, so kids will need to think a little differently in order to do well.

CogAT Screening Form Test Prep Book

Length

Students take about 30 minutes to complete the test.

Format

The Level 11 Grade 5 test is made up of 64 multiple choice questions.

Test Sections

Verbal Analogies: Students are provided with two words that form a pair, as well as a third word. From the answer choices, the student must select the word that goes with the third provided word.

Figure Matrices: Students are given a 2x2 matrix with the image missing in one cell. Students must determine the relationship between the two spatial forms in the top row and find a fourth image that has the same relationship to the spatial form in the bottom row.

Number Analogies: Students are provided with two sets of analogous numbers, and a third set with a missing number. To determine the missing number, students must find the relationship between the numbers in each of the first two sets, and apply it to the final set.

Part 2: How to Use this Book

The CogAT® Screening Form an important test and the more a student is familiar with the questions on the exam, the better she will fare when taking the test.

This book will help your student get used to the format & content of the test so s/he will be adequately prepared and feel confident on test day.

Inside this book, you will find:

- Sample question for each question type on the test and teaching tips to help your child approach each question type strategically and with confidence.

- Full-length CogAT® Level 11 Screening Form practice test.

Part 3. Test Prep Tips and Strategies

Firstly, and most importantly, commit to make the test preparation process a stress-free one. A student's ability to keep calm and focused in the face of challenge is a quality that will benefit her throughout her academic life.

Be prepared for difficult questions from the get-go! There will be a certain percentage of questions that are very challenging for all children. It is key to encourage students to use all strategies available when faced with challenging questions. And remember that a student can get quite a few questions wrong and still do very well on the test.

Before starting the practice test, go through the sample questions and read the teaching tips provided at the beginning of the book. They will help you guide your student as he or she progresses through the practice test.

The following strategies may also be useful as you help your child prepare:

Before You Start

Find a quiet, comfortable spot to work free of distractions. Show your student how to perform the simple technique of shading (and erasing) bubbles.

CogAT Screening Form Test Prep Book

During Prep

If your student is challenged by a question, ask your child to explain why he or she chose a specific answer. If the answer was incorrect, this will help you identify where your student is stumbling. If the answer was correct, asking your student to articulate her reasoning aloud will help reinforce the concept.

Encourage your student to carefully consider all the answer options before selecting one. Tell him or her there is only ONE correct answer.

If your student is stumped by a question, she or he can use the process of elimination. First, encourage your student to eliminate obviously wrong answers to narrow down the answer choices. If your student is still in doubt after using this technique, tell him or her to guess as there are no points deducted for wrong answers.

Review all the questions your student answered incorrectly, and explain to your student why the answer is incorrect. Have your student attempt these questions again a few days later to see if he now understands the concept.

Encourage your student to do her best, but take plenty of study breaks. Start with 15-20 minute sessions. Your student will perform best if she views these activities as fun and engaging, not as exercises to be avoided.

When to Start Preparing?

Every parent/teacher & student will approach preparation for this test differently. There is no 'right' way to prepare; there is only the best way for a particular student.

If you have limited time to prepare, spend most energy reviewing areas where your student is encountering the majority of problems.

As they say, knowledge is power! Preparing for the CogAT® will certainly help your student avoid anxiety and make sure she does not give up too soon when faced with unfamiliar and perplexing questions.

Verbal Analogies Question Sample and Tips

There are 24 Verbal Analogies questions in the CogAT® Level 11.

SAMPLE QUESTION:

Find the relationship between the first two words, then choose a word that has the same relationship with the third word.

teacher : student   as   doctor :

A. hospital   B. patient   C. passenger   D. medicine   E. customer

Correct Answer: B. A teacher helps students as a doctor helps patients.

TEACHING TIPS

- To master analogies, a student needs to have general background knowledge, and an understanding/recognition of various relationships, including:
  - → Object/function — One word in a pair describes the purpose or function of the other word.
  - → Agent (person or animal)/location.
  - → Agent (person or animal)/action.
  - → Definition/Evidence—One word in a pair helps to define the other word; or, one word in a pair is a defining characteristic of the other word.
  - → Synonym/Antonym—One word in a pair is a synonym or antonym of the other word.
  - → Degree/Intensity—Both words in a pair are similar in concept, but vary in intensity.
  - → Component/Part—One word in a pair represents one part of the other word, which represents a whole; or, one word is simply a component of the other.

- As often as possible, incorporate discussions about similarities, differences, and relationships between words into your everyday conversation with your student. Help your student begin thinking about how different words and concepts are connected to one another.

- When answering practice questions, teach your student to determine the relationship between the first pair of words before looking at the answer choices. Once your student determines the relationship between the first pair, she can then look at the answer choices to find the pair with the exact same relationship.

Figure Matrices Question Sample and Tips

There are 22 Figure Matrices questions in the CogAT® Level 11.

SAMPLE QUESTION:

Look at the shapes in the boxes on top. These shapes go together in a certain way. Which answer choice belongs where the question mark is?

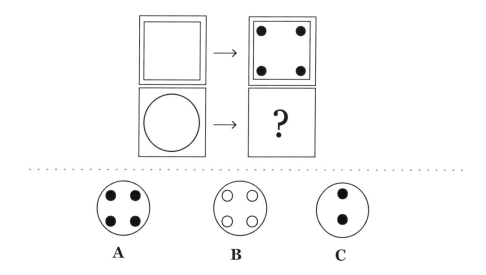

Correct Answer: **A.** In the top row, there are two figures that go together in a certain way. They go together in the sense that as the figure moves from left box to right box, it stays the same shape (a square) but adds four black circles inside.

Your student needs to find the figure among the answer options that fits best in the question mark box on the bottom row. The correct choice will have the same relationship with the figure on the bottom row that the figures in the top row have with each other.

Option B is incorrect because, although the figure is the same shape as the figure on the bottom row, the inside circles that are added are white. Option C is incorrect because, although the figure is the same shape as the figure on the bottom row, only two black inside circles are added. Option A is correct as the figure has the same shape (circle) as the figure on the bottom row and it has four black circles inside.

TEACHING TIPS

- Make sure your student knows key concepts that come up in these types of questions, including geometric concepts such as rotational symmetry, line symmetry, parts of a whole.

- If your student is finding these items difficult, encourage her to discover the pattern by isolating one element (e.g: outer shape, inner shape/s) and identify how it changes:

  → Ask: Is the color/shading of the element changing as it moves?

  → Ask: Is the element changing positions as it moves? Does it move up or down? Clockwise or counter-clockwise? Does it end up in the opposite (mirror) position?

  → Ask: Does the element disappear or increase in number as it moves along the row? Does it get bigger or smaller?

- Encourage your student to make a prediction for the missing object and compare the description with the answer choices.

Number Analogies Question Sample and Tips

There are 18 Number Analogies questions in the CogAT® Level 11.

SAMPLE QUESTION: Find the relationship between the numbers in the first set, and between the numbers in the second set. Then choose a number which follows the same pattern when paired with the number in the third set.

[10 → 2]   [20 → 4]   [30 → ?]

A. 3   B. 7   C. 6   D. 4   E. 10

Correct Answer: C. The rule is to divide the first number in each set by 5, so the answer is 6 (option C).

TEACHING TIPS

- Your child is probably not accustomed to completing number matrices, so it is important to frequently expose him to this question type in order to build confidence and familiarity.

- Consider modeling how to approach solving a number matrix by "thinking aloud" as you work through a question with your child.

- Work with your child on basic mathematical concepts, including addition, subtraction, division, multiplication.

COGAT® LEVEL 11
SCREENING FORM
PRACTICE TEST

VERBAL BATTERY

• • • • • • • • • • • • •

VERBAL ANALOGIES PRACTICE QUESTIONS

• • • • • • • • • • • • • • • • • • •

For each item, the student is presented with two words that have a relationship or go together in a particular way.

The student needs to figure out the relationship between those first two words. The student then needs to choose the word in the answer choices that has the same relationship with the third word.

VERBAL ANALOGIES

boxer : gloves as carpenter : ?

A. craft   **B.** tools   **C.** ant   **D.** fighter   **E.** table

frog: amphibian as koala : ?

A. tadpole   **B.** pouch   **C.** marsupial   **D.** tree   **E.** reptile

skiing : slope as driving : ?

A. car   **B.** glide   **C.** road   **D.** traffic   **E.** cross country

petite : tiny as obese : ?

A. slender   **B.** large   **C.** eating   **D.** person   **E.** small

saturn: planet as incisor : ?

A. measure   **B.** molar   **C.** mouth   **D.** solar   **E.** tooth

VERBAL ANALOGIES

6. **turkey : bird as cactus : ?**

   A. prickly   **B.** plant   **C.** desert   **D.** seaweed   **E.** water

7. **cyclist : track as swimmer: ?**

   A. race   **B.** driver   **C.** pool   **D.** goggles   **E.** swim

8. **hair stylist: salon as pilot : ?**

   A. cabin   **B.** scissors   **C.** wings   **D.** cockpit   **E.** ship

9. **librarian : library as bellhop: ?**

   A. books   **B.** work   **C.** profession   **D.** hotel   **E.** luggage

10. **consent : oppose as primitive : ?**

    A. surrender   **B.** infant   **C.** young   **D.** ancient   **E.** modern

VERBAL ANALOGIES

bright : brilliant as cry : ?

A. shine   B. tear   C. sob   D. smile   E. speak

vacant : empty as pupil : ?

A. school   B. eye   C. teacher   D. unoccupied   E. student

lion : cage as valuables : ?

A. money   B. jewelry   C. box   D. vault   E. zoo

gas tank : gas as bone : ?

A. car   B. marrow   C. flesh   D. leg   E. boney

provoke : soothe as loathe : ?

A. cherish   B. aggravate   C. detest   D. insult   E. win

16. **feet : yard as quart : ?**

    A. gallon   **B.** half   **C.** inch   **D.** kilometer   **E.** measureme

17. **debate : agree as excavate : ?**

    A. dig   **B.** dispute   **C.** consent   **D.** bury   **E.** scrape

18. **pencil : graphite as thermometer : ?**

    A. temperature   **B.** sick   **C.** mercury   **D.** lead   **E.** iodine

19. **rural : soil as urban : ?**

    A. city   **B.** skyscraper   **C.** pavement   **D.** sand   **E.** dirt

20. **breeze : gale as drip : ?**

    A. cascade   **B.** wash   **C.** storm   **D.** storm   **E.** fall

VERBAL ANALOGIES

. **pack : wolf as pod : ?**

   A. school   **B.** whale   **C.** fish   **D.** pea   **E.** class

. **desk : wood as tire : ?**

   A. material   **B.** rubber   **C.** car   **D.** plastic   **E.** drive

. **kangaroo : joey as bird : ?**

   A. blackbird   **B.** eaglet   **C.** fly   **D.** baby   **E.** fledgling

. **absurd : sensible as fatigue : ?**

   A. tired   **B.** crazy   **C.** liveliness   **D.** clumsy   **E.** exhausted

NON-VERBAL BATTERY

• • • • • • • • • • • •

FIGURE MATRICES

PRACTICE QUESTIONS

• •

Figure Matrices

Look at the shapes in the boxes on top. These shapes go together in a certain way. Which shape belongs where the question mark is?

1

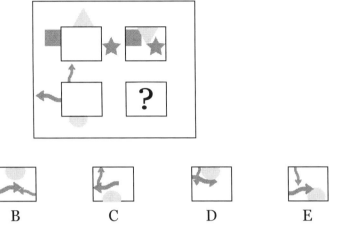

Look at the shapes in the boxes on top. These shapes go together in a certain way. Which shape belongs where the question mark is?

2

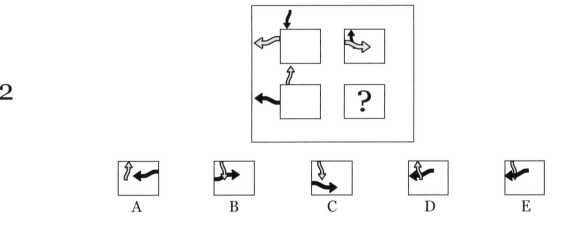

Look at the shapes in the boxes on top. These shapes go together in a certain way. Which shape belongs where the question mark is?

3

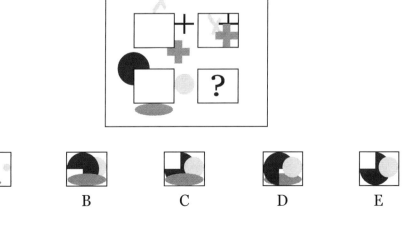

Figure Matrices

Look at the shapes in the boxes on top. These shapes go together in a certain way. Which shape belongs where the question mark is?

4

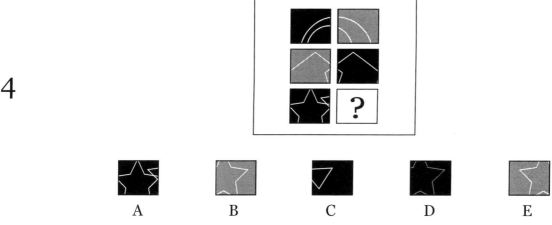

Look at the shapes in the boxes on top. These shapes go together in a certain way. Which shape belongs where the question mark is?

5

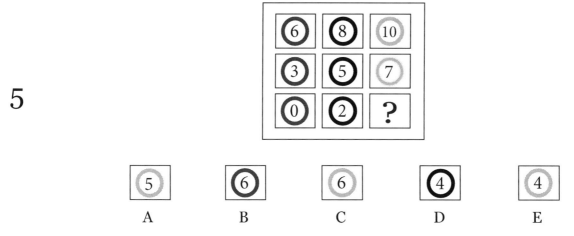

Look at the shapes in the boxes on top. These shapes go together in a certain way. Which shape belongs where the question mark is?

6

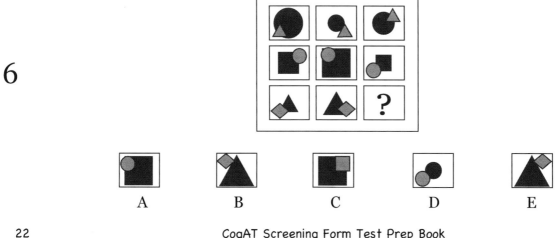

CogAT Screening Form Test Prep Book

Figure Matrices

Look at the shapes in the boxes on top. These shapes go together in a certain way. Which shape belongs where the question mark is?

7

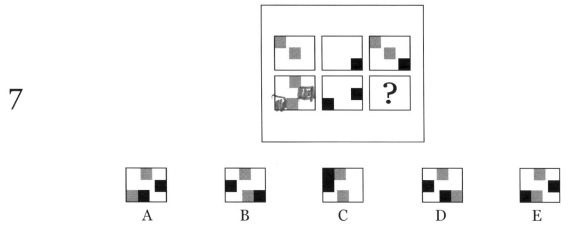

Look at the shapes in the boxes on top. These shapes go together in a certain way. Which shape belongs where the question mark is?

8

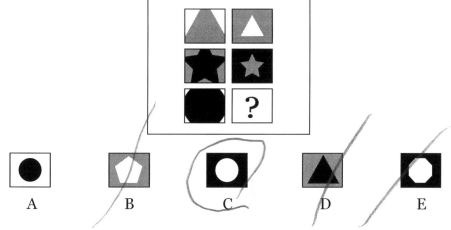

Look at the shapes in the boxes on top. These shapes go together in a certain way. Which shape belongs where the question mark is?

9

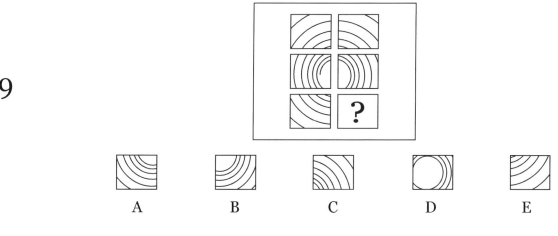

Figure Matrices

Look at the shapes in the boxes on top. These shapes go together in a certain way. Which shape belongs where the question mark is?

10

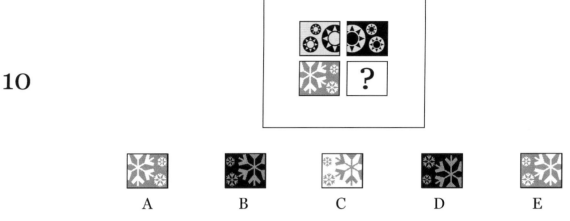

Look at the shapes in the boxes on top. These shapes go together in a certain way. Which shape belongs where the question mark is?

11

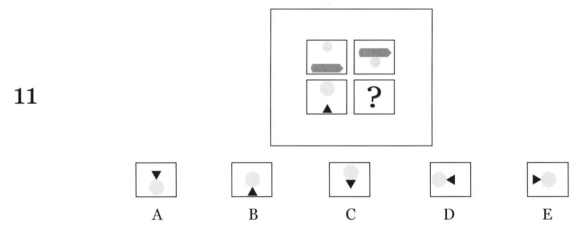

Look at the shapes in the boxes on top. These shapes go together in a certain way. Which shape belongs where the question mark is?

12

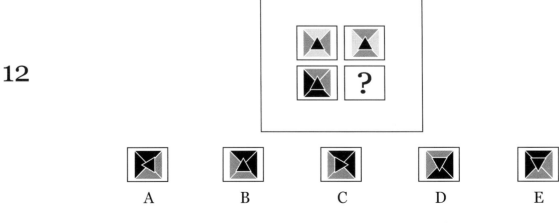

CogAT Screening Form Test Prep Book

Figure Matrices

Look at the shapes in the boxes on top. These shapes go together in a certain way. Which shape belongs where the question mark is?

13

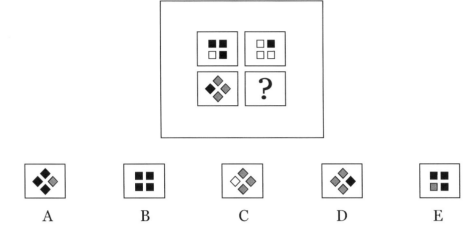

A B C D E

Look at the shapes in the boxes on top. These shapes go together in a certain way. Which shape belongs where the question mark is?

14

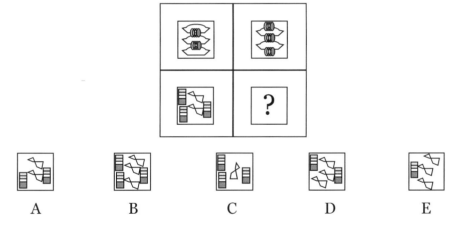

A B C D E

Look at the shapes in the boxes on top. These shapes go together in a certain way. Which shape belongs where the question mark is?

15

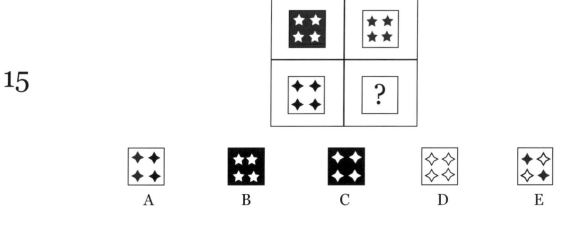

A B C D E

Figure Matrices

Look at the shapes in the boxes on top. These shapes go together in a certain way. Which shape belongs where the question mark is?

16

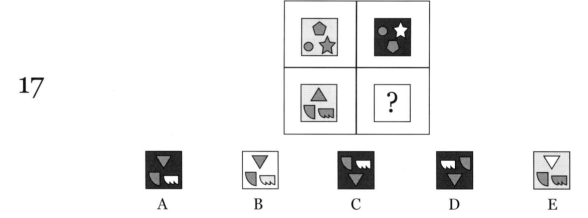

Look at the shapes in the boxes on top. These shapes go together in a certain way. Which shape belongs where the question mark is?

17

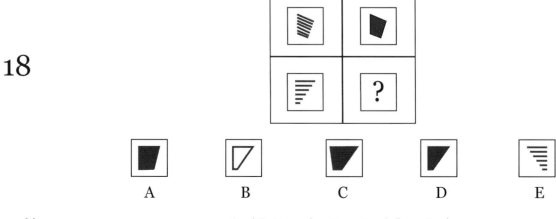

Look at the shapes in the boxes on top. These shapes go together in a certain way. Which shape belongs where the question mark is?

18

CogAT Screening Form Test Prep Book

Figure Matrices

Look at the shapes in the boxes on top. These shapes go together in a certain way. Which shape belongs where the question mark is?

19

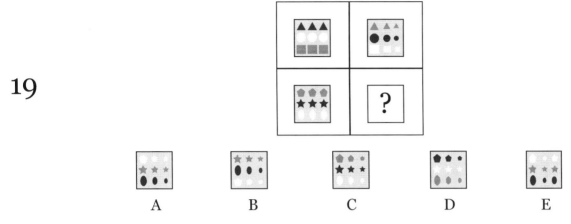

Look at the shapes in the boxes on top. These shapes go together in a certain way. Which shape belongs where the question mark is?

20

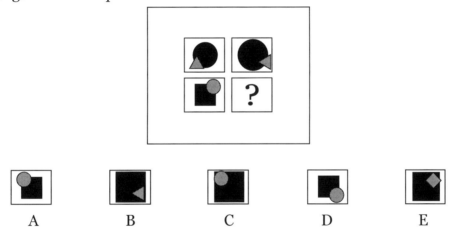

Look at the shapes in the boxes on top. These shapes go together in a certain way. Which shape belongs where the question mark is?

21

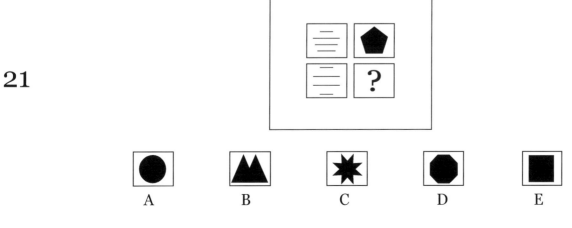

Look at the shapes in the boxes on top. These shapes go together in a certain way. Which shape belongs where the question mark is?

22

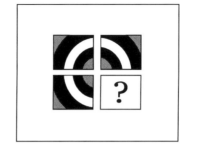

   A   B   C   D   E

QUANTITATIVE BATTERY

• • • • • • • • • •

NUMBER ANALOGIES PRACTICE QUESTIONS

• • • • • • • • • • • • • • • • • • • •

For each of the following items, the student is presented with two sets of numbers.

The student needs to find the relationship between those numbers and then choose a number from the answer choices which follows the same pattern when paired with the number in the third set.

NUMBER ANALOGIES

1. [7 ➡ 16]   [15 ➡ 24]   [25 ➡ ?]

    A. 7   **B.** 9   **C.** 34   **D.** 16   **E.** 24

2. [6 ➡ 36]   [8 ➡ 48]   [11 ➡ ?]

    A. 18   **B.** 58   **C.** 51   **D.** 66   **E.** 88

3. [9 ➡ 4 ½]   [6 ➡ 3]   [3 ➡ ?]

    A. 1 ½   **B.** 3   **C.** 2 ½   **D.** ½   **E.** 0

4. [50 ➡ 45]   [5 ➡ 0]   [30 ➡ ?]

    A. 45   **B.** 0   **C.** 15   **D.** 20   **E.** 25

5. [**10** ➡ **100**]   [**100** ➡ **1000**]   [**50** ➡ ?]

    A. 5000   **B.** 100   **C.** 500   **D.** 1000   **E.** 50,000

6.　[7 ➡ 49]　　[10 ➡ 100]　　[5 ➡ ?]

　　A. 30　　　　B. 35　　　　C. 50　　　　D. 25　　　　E. 250

7.　[4 ➡ 1]　　[16 ➡ 4]　　[8 ➡ ?]

　　A. 1　　　　B. 2　　　　C. 3　　　　D. 4　　　　E. 6

8.　[5 ➡ 5]　　[10 ➡ 10]　　[0 ➡ ?]

　　A. 0　　　　B. 5　　　　C. 10　　　　D. 100　　　　E. 1

9.　[2 ➡ 4]　　[4 ➡ 16]　　[6 ➡ ?]

　　A. 25　　　　B. 36　　　　C. 8　　　　D. 18　　　　E. 42

10.　[2 ➡ 14]　　[4 ➡ 28]　　[7 ➡ ?]

　　A. 12　　　　B. 22　　　　C. 7　　　　D. 49　　　　E. 56

NUMBER ANALOGIES

1. [1 ➡ 1 ¾]   [1 ¾ ➡ 2 ½]   [2 ½ ➡ ?]

   A. 2 ¾   **B.** 3 ¼   **C.** 4 ¼   **D.** 3 ½   **E.** 3

2. [8 ➡ 13]   [4 ➡ 9]   [10 ➡ ?]

   A. 14   **B.** 18   **C.** 12   **D.** 17   **E.** 15

3. [½ ➡ ¼]   [¼ ➡ 0]   [1 ➡ ?]

   A. ¼   **B.** ½   **C.** ¾   **D.** 1 ¼   **E.** 0

4. [1 ➡ 100]   [10 ➡ 10000]   [0 ➡ ?]

   A. 1000   **B.** 10   **C.** 0   **D.** 1   **E.** 100

5. [2/4 ➡ ½]   [3/6 ➡ ½]   [4/8 ➡ ?]

   A. ½   **B.** ⅓   **C.** 2/8   **D.** 2/6   **E.** ¼

NUMBER ANALOGIES

16.   [40   ➡   28]   [30   ➡   18]   [20   ➡   ?]

     A. 8   **B.** 12   **C.** 18   **D.** 28   **E.** 7

17.   [36   ➡   12]   [30   ➡   10]   [6   ➡   ?]

     A. 4   **B.** 2   **C.** 4   **D.** 10   **E.** 6

18.   [0.01   ➡   0.1]   [0.002   ➡   0.02]   [0.3   ➡   ?]

     A. 0.003   **B.** 0.03   **C.** 3   **D.** 0.4   **E.** 30

Answer Explanations

Verbal Analogies

1. **B**. A boxer uses gloves as a carpenter uses tools.

2. **C**. Frogs belong to the amphibian class of animals as koalas belong to the marsupial class of animals.

3. **C**. Skiing is performed on a slope as driving is done on a road.

4. **B**. 'Petite' and 'tiny' are synonyms as 'obese' and 'large' are synonyms.

5. **E**. Saturn is an example of a planet as an incisor is a type of tooth.

6. **B**. A turkey is a type of a bird as a cactus is a type of plant.

7. **C**. A cyclist rides a bicycle on a track as a swimmer swims in a pool.

8. **D**. A hairstylist works in a salon as a pilot works in the cockpit of a plane.

9. **D**. A librarian works in a library as a bellhop works in a hotel.

10. **E**. 'Consent' and 'oppose' are antonyms as 'primitive' and 'modern' are antonyms.

11. **C**. 'Bright' and 'brilliant' are synonyms as 'sob' and 'cry' are synonyms.

12. **E**. 'Vacant' and 'empty' are synonyms as 'pupil' and 'student' are synonyms.

13. **D**. A lion can be kept in a cage like valuables can be kept in a vault.

14. **B**. A gas tank holds gas like a bone holds marrow.

15. **A**. 'Provoke' and 'soothe' are antonyms as 'loathe' and 'cherish' are antonyms.

16. **A**. Feet are units of measurement that make up yards and quarts are units of measurement that make up gallons.

17. **D**. 'Debate' and 'agree' are antonyms as 'excavate' and 'bury' are antonyms.

18. **C**. A pencil contains graphite as a thermometer contains mercury.

19. **C**. Rural areas have a lot of open land and soil as urban areas have a lot of roads and pavement.

20. **A**. A breeze is a very light wind and a gale is a very strong wind as a drip is a small drop of liquid and a cascade is a downpour.

21. **B**. A pack is a group of wolves as a pod is a group of whales.

22. **B**. A desk is composed of wood as a tire is composed of rubber.

23. **E**. A joey is a baby kangaroo as a fledgling is a baby bird.

24. **C**. 'Absurd' and 'sensible' are antonyms as 'fatigue' and 'liveliness' are antonyms.

Figure Matrices

1. **A**. The shapes are folded inward.

2. **B**. The black arrow folds in first, then the light gray arrow folds in.

3. **C**. The shapes are folded inward.

4. **B**. The correct box completes the mural of two stars in the bottom row while the background shades alternate.

5. **E**. Across each row, the outer circles change shades as the numbers increase by 2, Down the columns, the numbers decrease by 3 from top to bottom.

6. **E**. The black shapes alternate between large, medium and small, while the foreground shapes (medium gray) move counterclockwise around the black shape.

7. **E**. In each row, the squares from column 1 combine with the squares from column 2 to become column 3.

8. **C**. The shape is reduced while the shades are inverted.

9. **E**. The lines complete the spiral mural.

10. **C**. In the second column, the figures are reflected vertically and the colors are inverted.

11. **A**. The figures meet at the horizon and then reflect on the horizon.

12. **B**. The background shapes invert colors/ shades, while the topmost shape remains the same.

13. **A**. The figures are rotated 180 degrees, and the colors/shades are inverted.

14. **D**. Moving from the left to right box in the top row, the shape with three igures decreases by one and the shape with two igures (colored/shaded rings) increases by one. The bottom boxes must re lect the same relationship.

15. **C**. Moving from left to right box, the color of the background and inner shapes are inverted.

16. **E**. In the left box are three triangles and three arrowheads. Moving from the left to right box, the position of the arrowheads are left undisturbed, but the colors/shades of the arrowheads are inverted. The set of three triangles rotates 180 degrees but the triangles' shades/colors are retained.

17. **C**. Moving from the left to right box, the background color/shade changes to black, the shape at the top moves to the bottom and it is rotated 180 degrees. The shape at the bottom right changes color to white and moves to the top, the shape at the bottom left retains its color/shade and moves to the top.

18. **D**. Moving from the left to right box, the lines form a shape filled with black.

19. **A**. Moving from the left to right box, the black)changes to medium gray,white changes to black, and medium gray changes to white. The size of the left column of shapes remains the same, while the shapes in the middle column becomes medium sized, and the shapes in the right column becomes small sized.

20. **C**. The shapes rotate 80 degrees counterclockwise while the background image increases in size.

21. **D**. The lines in the left column, if surrounded by an outside line, form the shape in the right column.

22. **E**. The bottom right figure completes the larger mural.

Number Analogies

1. **C**. Add 9

2. **D**. Multiply by 6

3. **A**. Divide by 2

4. **E**. Subtract 5

5. **C**. Multiply by 10

6. **D**. Square each number

7. **B**. Divide by 4

8. **A**. Subtract 0 from each number

9. **B**. Square each number

10. **D**. Multiply by 7

11. **B**. Add ¾

12. **E**. Add 5

13. **C**. Subtract ¼

14. **C**. Multiply by 100

15. **A**. Equivalent to ½

16. **A**. Subtract 12

17. **B**. Divide by 3

18. **C**. Multiply by 10

CogAT® Bubble Sheet

Use a No. 2 Pencil
Fill in bubble completely.

Ⓐ ● Ⓒ Ⓓ

Name:_____

Date:_____

1. Ⓐ Ⓑ Ⓒ Ⓓ Ⓔ	1. Ⓐ Ⓑ Ⓒ Ⓓ Ⓔ	1. Ⓐ Ⓑ Ⓒ Ⓓ Ⓔ
2. Ⓐ Ⓑ Ⓒ Ⓓ Ⓔ	2. Ⓐ Ⓑ Ⓒ Ⓓ Ⓔ	2. Ⓐ Ⓑ Ⓒ Ⓓ Ⓔ
3. Ⓐ Ⓑ Ⓒ Ⓓ Ⓔ	3. Ⓐ Ⓑ Ⓒ Ⓓ Ⓔ	3. Ⓐ Ⓑ Ⓒ Ⓓ Ⓔ
4. Ⓐ Ⓑ Ⓒ Ⓓ Ⓔ	4. Ⓐ Ⓑ Ⓒ Ⓓ Ⓔ	4. Ⓐ Ⓑ Ⓒ Ⓓ Ⓔ
5. Ⓐ Ⓑ Ⓒ Ⓓ Ⓔ	5. Ⓐ Ⓑ Ⓒ Ⓓ Ⓔ	5. Ⓐ Ⓑ Ⓒ Ⓓ Ⓔ
6. Ⓐ Ⓑ Ⓒ Ⓓ Ⓔ	6. Ⓐ Ⓑ Ⓒ Ⓓ Ⓔ	6. Ⓐ Ⓑ Ⓒ Ⓓ Ⓔ
7. Ⓐ Ⓑ Ⓒ Ⓓ Ⓔ	7. Ⓐ Ⓑ Ⓒ Ⓓ Ⓔ	7. Ⓐ Ⓑ Ⓒ Ⓓ Ⓔ
8. Ⓐ Ⓑ Ⓒ Ⓓ Ⓔ	8. Ⓐ Ⓑ Ⓒ Ⓓ Ⓔ	8. Ⓐ Ⓑ Ⓒ Ⓓ Ⓔ
9. Ⓐ Ⓑ Ⓒ Ⓓ Ⓔ	9. Ⓐ Ⓑ Ⓒ Ⓓ Ⓔ	9. Ⓐ Ⓑ Ⓒ Ⓓ Ⓔ
10. Ⓐ Ⓑ Ⓒ Ⓓ Ⓔ	10. Ⓐ Ⓑ Ⓒ Ⓓ Ⓔ	10. Ⓐ Ⓑ Ⓒ Ⓓ Ⓔ
11. Ⓐ Ⓑ Ⓒ Ⓓ Ⓔ	11. Ⓐ Ⓑ Ⓒ Ⓓ Ⓔ	11. Ⓐ Ⓑ Ⓒ Ⓓ Ⓔ
12. Ⓐ Ⓑ Ⓒ Ⓓ Ⓔ	12. Ⓐ Ⓑ Ⓒ Ⓓ Ⓔ	12. Ⓐ Ⓑ Ⓒ Ⓓ Ⓔ
13. Ⓐ Ⓑ Ⓒ Ⓓ Ⓔ	13. Ⓐ Ⓑ Ⓒ Ⓓ Ⓔ	13. Ⓐ Ⓑ Ⓒ Ⓓ Ⓔ
14. Ⓐ Ⓑ Ⓒ Ⓓ Ⓔ	14. Ⓐ Ⓑ Ⓒ Ⓓ Ⓔ	14. Ⓐ Ⓑ Ⓒ Ⓓ Ⓔ
15. Ⓐ Ⓑ Ⓒ Ⓓ Ⓔ	15. Ⓐ Ⓑ Ⓒ Ⓓ Ⓔ	15. Ⓐ Ⓑ Ⓒ Ⓓ Ⓔ
16. Ⓐ Ⓑ Ⓒ Ⓓ Ⓔ	16. Ⓐ Ⓑ Ⓒ Ⓓ Ⓔ	16. Ⓐ Ⓑ Ⓒ Ⓓ Ⓔ
17. Ⓐ Ⓑ Ⓒ Ⓓ Ⓔ	17. Ⓐ Ⓑ Ⓒ Ⓓ Ⓔ	17. Ⓐ Ⓑ Ⓒ Ⓓ Ⓔ
18. Ⓐ Ⓑ Ⓒ Ⓓ Ⓔ	18. Ⓐ Ⓑ Ⓒ Ⓓ Ⓔ	18. Ⓐ Ⓑ Ⓒ Ⓓ Ⓔ
19. Ⓐ Ⓑ Ⓒ Ⓓ Ⓔ	19. Ⓐ Ⓑ Ⓒ Ⓓ Ⓔ	
20. Ⓐ Ⓑ Ⓒ Ⓓ Ⓔ	20. Ⓐ Ⓑ Ⓒ Ⓓ Ⓔ	
21. Ⓐ Ⓑ Ⓒ Ⓓ Ⓔ	21. Ⓐ Ⓑ Ⓒ Ⓓ Ⓔ	
22. Ⓐ Ⓑ Ⓒ Ⓓ Ⓔ	22. Ⓐ Ⓑ Ⓒ Ⓓ Ⓔ	
23. Ⓐ Ⓑ Ⓒ Ⓓ Ⓔ		
24. Ⓐ Ⓑ Ⓒ Ⓓ Ⓔ		

Made in the USA
Middletown, DE
10 November 2019